T0163096

NABOKOV IN 90 MINUTES

Nabokov
IN 90 MINUTES

Paul Strathern

IVAN R. DEE
CHICAGO

www.ivanrdee.com

Library of Congress Cataloging-in-Publication Data:
Strathern, Paul, 1940–
    Nabokov in 90 minutes / Paul Strathern.
        p. cm. — (Great writers in 90 minutes)
    Includes bibliographical references (p.) and index.
    ISBN 1-56663-589-6 (acid-free paper) —
    ISBN 1-56663-590-X (pbk. : acid-free paper)
    1. Nabokov, Vladimir Vladimirovich, 1899–1977. 2. Authors, Russian—20th century—Biography. 3. Authors, American—20th century—Biography. I. Title: Nabokov in ninety minutes. II. Title.
    PG3476.N3Z88 2005
    813'.54—dc22
                                                    2004056921

Contents

NABOKOV IN 90 MINUTES

Introduction

Vladimir Nabokov's early life was marred by two formative events. On October 24, 1917, the provisional Russian government in which his father was serving was overthrown by the Bolshevik Revolution. Back home that night, the dandified eighteen-year-old Nabokov continued composing a series of love poems to two different girls, but noted later: "As I was writing, fierce rifle fire and the foul crackle of a machine gun could be heard from the street." Next morning, Nabokov rose as usual and set about his daily exercises, sparring with a punchball in his father's library, seemingly oblivious of the occasional gunfire outside in the street. Several armed soldiers broke in through the window, but the butler managed to persuade them that the young man was not a Cossack preparing to ambush them, and escorted them from the room. Nabokov bathed and dressed, then went down to the courtyard, where the family chauffeur and Rolls Royce were waiting to drive him and his younger brother Sergey to school.

Five years later the Nabokov family were living in exile in Berlin. Nabokov's father was running the exile Russian-language newspaper *Rul'* (The Rudder), which propagated moderate views, condemning both the excesses of the Russian revolutionaries and the extreme right-wing views of the exiled tsarists. On March 28, 1922, Nabokov's father appeared at a public meeting alongside Paul Miliukov, a leader of the moderate faction. Nabokov, now twenty-two, had no interest in such meetings and did not attend. He and his brother Sergey were on holiday from Cambridge University in England, where their fees were being paid by the pearls his mother had managed to smuggle out of Russia when they had fled the revolution.

That March day in 1922 Berlin, the young Vladimir Nabokov recorded in his diary: "I returned home about 9 pm, after a heavenly day. After dinner I sat in the chair by the divan and opened a little volume of Blok. Mother, half-lying, was setting the cards out for patience. . . . I was reading aloud those tender poems about Italy, about damp, resonant Venice, about Florence, like a smoky iris." The phone rang in the hall, and he went out to answer it, "annoyed that my reading was interrupted."

As a consequence of this phone call, Nabokov learned that the meeting attended by his father had broken up amidst sensational circumstances. An assassin had leapt onto the stage with the intenton of shooting Miliukov. Nabokov's father had realized what was happening and had struggled with the assassin. A second assassin, the fanatical tsarist Sergey Taboritsky, had then shot Nabokov's father, apparently mistaking him for Miliukov. The assassination attempt had failed, but Nabokov's father was dead.

Nabokov was devastated. He had idolized his father and had been very close to him, despite their differing interests. First the Nabokovs had been forced into exile, now the family was dispersed. Nabokov's mother and sisters went to live in Prague, his brother Sergey went to Paris. After graduating from Cambridge, Nabokov himself returned to live in Berlin, where he eked out an existence writing novels and short stories in Russian. In 1936 his father's assassin Sergey Taboritsky was appointed by the Nazis to a post overseeing the Russian emigré community in Berlin, and Nabokov fled to Paris with his half-Jewish wife and their two-year-old son. When his mother became fatally ill 1938, he was unable to afford the fare to see her. Two years later, as the Nazis overran France, Nabokov managed to obtain a berth to America for himself and his family on the last passenger liner to leave France. His brother Sergey, who had been out of Paris at the time and was left behind, would eventually die in a concentration camp. At the age of forty-one Nabokov arrived in America virtually penniless, an unknown writer with a family to support. Amongst his luggage was the manuscript of a failed novella called *Volshebnik* (The Enchanter), which featured a middle-aged man with a passion for a twelve-year-old girl who would eventually be given the name Lolita.

Nabokov's Life and Works

Vladimir Nabokov was the scion of a distinguished Russian family. His great-granduncle, General Ivan Nabokov, had fought against the the Napoleonic army at the Battle of Borodino in 1812 and was later made governor of the notorious Peter and Paul Fortress in St. Petersburg, where one of his prisoners was Dostoevsky. Vladimir Nabokov's paternal grandfather, Dmitri Nabokov, served under no less than three tsars as minister of justice, though this post was something of an oxymoron during such autocratic times. As a result, his mildly liberal views led to him being dismissed by the tyrannical Tsar Alexander III. The rich and sophisticated

Nabokov family would become known for their liberal views. These would come to the fore with Nabokov's father, V. D. Nabokov, who in 1906 became a member of the first democratically elected Duma (Russian parliament). When Tsar Nicholas II took the unconstitutional step of dissolving the Duma, V. D. Nabokov was instrumental in assembling the dismissed Duma at Viborg in defiance of the tsar. For this role he would serve three months in prison in 1908 and be banned from all political activity. Nine years later when the tsar was deposed, V. D. Nabokov was appointed a minister in the short-lived provisional government, which would be deposed by Lenin and the Bolsheviks in October 1917.

V. D. Nabokov's son Vladimir Vladimirovich Nabokov, was born in St. Petersburg on April 10, 1899. After the reform of the Russian calendar and various documentary errors, Nabokov's birthday became April 23, which as Nabokov was keen to point out was "also the birthdate of Shakespeare [and] Shirley Temple [the famous curly-haired child film star]." Nabokov grew up amidst the cultured and privileged surroundings expected of one of Russia's leading families, spending the glittering winter "season" in the capital St. Petersburg and passing the summer months amidst the rural idyll of the family country estates. As the firstborn, young Volodya was worshiped by his mother and father from the word go. And the arrival of consequent brothers and sisters would not dislodge him from the favored position. This would result in a strong element of narcissism in his character, which later affected his writing. Only the poignancy of all that Narcissus had lost would redeem this quality. His concentration upon the minutiae of the childhood land from which exile had excluded him forever, and the childish emotions this evoked, would produce his autobiographical masterpiece *Speak, Memory*. This book is filled with a juvenile self-delight peculiarly appropriate to such memories, even if its style does occasionally tend to rose-tinted prose:

> An inexperienced heraldist resembles a medieval traveller who brings back from the East the faunal fantasies influenced by the

domestic bestiary he possessed all along rather than by the results of direct zoological exploration. Thus, in the first verion of this chapter, when describing the Nabokovs' coat of arms (carelessly glimpsed among some familial trivia many years before), I somehow managed to twist it into the fireside wonder of two bears posing with a great chessboard propped between them. . . .

In *Speak, Memory*, Nabokov evokes everything from the family crest to the family eyebrows and nose: "The Nabokov nose (e.g. my grandfather's) is of the Russian type with a soft round upturned tip and a gentle inslope in profile." Only the most convinced egoist, whose conviction extends into stylish literary self-awareness, can carry off such intimate scrutiny without inflicting verbal halitosis. The exhibitionist must at all times be fully aware of the exhibition he is making of himself, and Nabokov mostly succeeds in this delicately balanced dual role. He aptly characterizes this tale of his childhood as "my private footpath which runs parallel to the road of that troubled decade." But this private footpath should not be mistaken for an accurate rendition of past actuality, despite Nabokov's claims to the contrary. He was, as we all tend to do, remembering only precisely what he wanted to remember. The evocation is colored by the total loss inflicted by exile: he can never return, even to the site of the past. Each flawed crystal of memory is polished into a jewel. Nabokov was not false to his memory, he merely wished to evoke all that he so painfully missed. Unpolishable unpleasantness was for the most part glossed over. The presence of such blemishes can on occasion be detected if we scrutinize the text—even jewels cast tiny shadows. This was a problem that would come to affect Nabokov's later, greater works, of which *Speak, Memory* is certainly one.

Nabokov's childhood was cosseted by a team of valets, servants, governesses, gardeners, and so forth, who ministered to the family in its palatial St. Petersburg mansion and its extensive rural estates. (The children of these attendants acted as ball boys during the young masters' tennis games.) In such households, the governesses who looked after the children were likely to be imported from England, France, or Switzerland, and were unable to speak Russian. Nabokov's parents would speak to them fluently in their own language. As Nabokov himself put it, "I was a perfectly normal trilingual child." The governesses accompanied the family on their continental holidays to such established international watering holes as Biarritz or Wiesbaden. Nabokov's evocation of the long first-class railway journeys across Europe contain all the wonder and delight of this privileged bygone mode of transport.

> At a collapsible table, my mother and I played a card game called *durachki*. Although it was broad daylight, our cards, a glass, and, on a different plane, the locks of a suitcase were reflected in the window. Through forest and field, and in sudden ravines, and among scuttling cottages, those discarnate gamblers kept steadily playing on for steadily sparkling stakes.

As Nabokov grew up, the governesses gave way to private tutors. His father busied himself with running his political party, the Kadets, but still found time to pass on to his favorite son and heir his love of collecting butterflies, demonstrating his passion for preserving and mounting the collected specimens in the proper scientific fashion. This became part of the deep personal bond between father and son. When Nabokov's father was in prison, he was deeply touched to receive a butterfly from his nine-year-old son, and wrote to Nabokov's mother: "Tell him there are no butterflies here in the prison yard except *rhamni* and *P.brassicae*. Have you found any *egerias*?" Interestingly, this paternal yet exacting tone would also inform Nabokov's later literary style.

So what did Nabokov leave out in his description of his childhood? Certainly he includes references to what reached him from the "parallel . . . road of that troubled decade." The twelve-year-old Nabokov was aware that "The reactionary press never ceased to attack my father's party, and I had got quite used to the more or less vulgar cartoons which appeared from time to time—my father and Miliukov handing over Saint Russia on a plate to World Jewry and that sort of thing." He mentions his father's imprisonment and his worry over a duel that his father eventually did not have to fight. No, the trouble here is that *Speak, Memory* was a work of art, and was intended as such. As a result, starkness of emotion, unresolved complexities, and the ugly undigested gobbets which make up a young life tend to be missing, or at best dismissed with a mellifluous meticulousness. Childhood life can be turned into a work of art, but it is not one in itself. There is an elusive missing element—though this will only disappoint the pedant for actuality. As Nabokov himself put it, the word "reality" must always be used with inverted commas. So what we have in *Speak, Memory* is Nabokov's "childhood," with uglier truths appearing in the merest hints and asides: "I was more puzzled than pleased one day when upon hearing that I had deliberately slashed my leg above the knee with a razor blade (I still bear the scar) in order to avoid a recitation in class for which I was unprepared, [my father] seemed unable to work up any real wrath; and his subsequent admission of a parallel transgression in his own boyhood rewarded me for not withholding the truth." Seldom has an act of savage self-mutilation been so skillfully passed over.

Inevitably, school was not a pleasant experience for Nabokov. Solipsistic children seldom surrender gracefully to the polipsistic world of their peers. At the age of eleven, Nabokov was sent to the private Tenishev School, which was nonetheless a comparatively liberal establishment. His daily arrival in the family Rolls Royce inevitably set him apart from his fellows; yet when a kindly master suggested that he get out of the car a few blocks away so that "my schoolmates might be spared the sight of a liveried chauffeur doffing his cap," Nabokov chose to ignore this advice. He would continue to do things his way throughout his time at school. His well-coached intellectual abilities ensured that he coasted through the academic requirements, and he disdained to take part in extracurricular activities such as debates or societies. He had his own interests at home—lepidoptery, chess, poetry, and long, lost hours in his father's library. Even in the unavoidable games of soccer, he managed to keep aloof, choosing to play as goalkeeper, a solitary position for which few volunteered. Set apart from the rough and tumble of the game itself, he relished the opportunity to show off with acrobatic saves, becoming a fairly skilled 'keeper—though never quite accepted as one of the team.

In *Speak, Memory*, Nabokov freely admits that in his youth he was "a brittle young fop." This alone does not endear us, though Nabokov remains confident that the begrudging reader will be lulled into admiration by the verbal evidence of his superior mind—which even then, alone between the goalposts on a muddy afternoon, he would have been pensively putting through its paces. By his teenage years Nabokov was writing precociously accomplished poetry which lacked but one essential ingredient: originality. Nabokov's ability to mimic would prove another formative element of his mature style. In time this ability, with attendant ironies, erudition, and playful parody, would transcend its humble quasi-plagiaristic beginnings to achieve its own unimpeachable originality.

According to Nabokov: "Between the ages of ten and fifteen in St. Petersburg, I must have read more fiction and poetry—English, Russian, and French—than in any other five-year period of my life. I relished especially the works of Wells, Poe, Browning, Keats, Flaubert, Verlaine, Rimbaud, Chekhov, Tolstoy, and Alexander Blok." Little wonder that he had difficulty in finding a voice of his own. During the lazy weeks of summer in the country, after butterfly hunting all morning, he would spend the rainy afternoons or long pale evenings in the library of Uncle "Ruka," his mother's wealthy brother Vasily Rukavishnikov, who lived on the nearby estate of Rozhestveno. The Rukavishnikov country residence was a grand house, complete with imposing pillared porticoes, which had been designed by the architect of the tsar's Winter Palace and was set in its own two-thousand-acre estate.

Nabokov also found time for a number of puppy-love infatuations for pubescent girls from nearby families, who would attend name-day picnics in long white dresses. He developed particularly intense feelings for a girl called Polenka. One day he was out hunting butterflies:

> My quest led me into a dense undergrowth of milky-white racemosa and dark alder at the very edge of the cold, blue river, when suddenly there was an outburst of splashes and shouts, and from behind a fragrant bush, I caught sight of Polenka and three or four other naked children bathing from the ruins of an old bathhouse a few feet away. Wet, gasping, one nostril of her snub nose running, the ribs of her adolescent body arched under her pale, goose-pimpled skin, her calves flecked with black mud, a curved comb burning in her damp-darkened hair, she was scrambling away from the swish and clack of water-lily stems. . . .

Under such circumstances, it comes as little surprise that for Nabokov the outbreak of World War I in August 1914 passed as little more than a distant rumble of thunder on an otherwise glorious summer's day as he pursued his muse in a haze of poetry and love. (In contrast to Freud's belief that artistic inspiration was a sublimation of the sexual impulse, Nabokov always maintained that for him the two went hand in hand.)

Nabokov's father was mobilized into the army, but otherwise life went on much as ever chez Nabokov. In the summer of 1915, the sixteen-year-old Nabokov fell in love with a fifteen-year-old girl whose family was renting a nearby dacha. In *Speak, Memory*, Nabokov calls her "Tamara . . . a name concolorous with her real one" which was Liussya. Nabokov embarked upon a period of frenzied poetry-writing and accompanying rampant desires. In accord with his psychological theory, he led his muse by the hand to ever more secluded rural spots where he would read to her his poetic fantasies. "In one particular pine grove everything fell into place, I parted the fabric of fantasy, I touched reality." This unique reality apparently had no need of protective inverted commas. (While

Nabokov deflowered himself, unbeknown to the two lovers his tutor spied on them from the bushes with his telescope.)

After declaiming his love poems to Tamara, Nabokov would read them—adopting a more objective manner—to his admiring mother. When father returned from the front, he found himself less impressed by his son's poems. Summoning Nabokov to his study, he exclaimed: "What? You filled that girl?" There followed a tardy post facto lecture on how not to get a young girl, or himself, or both, into trouble.

Despite this somewhat mundane paternal interpretation of his work, Nabokov now gathered his more presentable poems together and had them privately published at his own expense in an edition of five hundred copies. This act of hubris prompted his headmaster, himself an accomplished minor poet, to vent his spleen on his precocious rival by devoting an entire literature lesson to pointing out the asinine dissonances and derivative assonances in Nabokov's poesy. Ironically, this was by way of being a considerable accolade. Just seven years earlier the same master had provided a similar service to another Tenishev School pupil, Osip Mandelstam, who was already being recognized as a leading poet of the brilliant new generation of "Russian Nightingales."

Either way, Nabokov adopted a pose of aloofness to the critical opinions of others, one which he would maintain throughout his literary career. (This attitude is exemplified in one of his novels, when the famous philosopher Adam Krug hears himself characterized as one of just a handful of renowned figures produced by his small country, whereupon he inquires, "Who are the other stars of this mysterious constellation?")

In 1916, Nabokov learned of the death of his Uncle Vasily, a bachelor who had favored wearing a violet carnation in his buttonhole. As a child Nabokov had been lifted onto his uncle's knee and furtively fumbled him in the process. Later Uncle Vasily's feelings had evidently blossomed into a platonic passion which he had kept to himself, for when he died he left his porticoed country mansion, the entire two-thousand-acre Rozhestveno estate, and a considerable fortune to his beloved seventeen-year-old nephew.

By now the war was going badly for Russia. The German blockade was causing widespread hunger in St. Petersberg. Things came to a head when those waiting in the food lines began calling for the overthrow of the tsar. In quick succession the Cossacks refused to disperse the starving crowds, the military garrison mutinied, and a provisional government was established. In February 1917, Tsar Nicholas II was forced to abdicate. The Kadets (short for Constitutional Democrats) played a major role in the provisional government, and Nabokov's father became a leading political figure. After a summer of civic turmoil in the capital, with the government becoming increasingly ineffectual, in October 1917 Lenin and the Bolsheviks seized power. Sensing the danger, Nabokov's father sent the family by rail fourteen hundred miles south to the safety of the Crimea. Later that month Nabokov's father was briefly arrested, and freed. Lenin then declared the Kadets "the party of the people's enemies" and issued an order for the detention and trial of its leaders. That evening Nabokov's father managed to obtain one of the last seats on a train leaving for the Crimea, and escaped with his life.

The Nabokovs spent a year and a half in the temperate Black Sea climate of the Crimea. Like the many other exiles who had fled the Bolshevik Revolution, they were forced to survive on money and jewelry which they (and their loyal servants) had brought with them. Nabokov's father had earlier been advised to transfer funds out of Russia, in case of just such an emergency, but he had patriotically refused to do such a thing in the midst of a war. Political circumstances in the Crimea remained uncertain and volatile, but the Nabokovs were for the most part unmolested in the series of holiday villas they inhabited.

With the coming of spring, Nabokov was pleased to record the catching of his first Crimean butterfly. But the Nabokovs eventually lost their last toehold in southern Russia and were forced to flee their homeland forever. In

Speak, Memory, Nabokov vividly records his last moments before a lifetime of exile:

> In March of 1919, the Reds broke through in nothern Crimea, and from various ports a tumultuous evacuation of anti-Bolshevik groups began. Over a glassy sea in the bay of Sebastopol, under wild machine-gun fire from the shore (the Bolshevik troops had just taken the port), my family and I set out for Constantinople and Piraeus on a small and shoddy Greek ship *Nadezhda* (Hope) carrying a cargo of dried fruit. I remember trying to concentrate, as we were zigzagging out of the bay, on a game of chess with my father. . . .

The family eventually settled in Berlin, which soon had a Russian exile population of more than 200,000, the largest in Europe. Nabokov was sent to school at Trinity College, Cambridge; his brother Sergey was sent to Oxford, though he soon left and decided to join his brother at Cambridge. It had now become clear that Sergey was a homosexual; the two brothers were awkward in each other's company, and apart from playing as tennis partners, for the most part they went their separate ways. Nabokov was painfully and almost constantly conscious of his exile and all that he had lost. Letters from "Tamara," written from her own exile in some remote Ukrainian village, had followed Nabokov to the Crimea; now they could no longer reach him. Uncle Vasily's country mansion and the estate Nabokov had inherited were nothing but a memory.

Although Nabokov had spoken English as a second language, the English themselves remained alien to him. Despite this he managed to strike up friendships with various English undergraduates, many of whom had also found their lives overwhelmed by historical circumstances—in their case the horrors of the trenches in the world war. In particular, Nabokov was drawn to the pipe-smoking young socialist veteran and versifier whom he called Nesbitt in *Speak, Memory*— in fact this was R. A. Butler, who would later become the Conservative deputy prime minister. Nabokov's sporting prowess brought him recognition of sorts, and he became goalkeeper for a college soccer team. In *Speak, Memory*, he notes of Cambridge:

> I remember the dreamy flow of punts and canoes on the Cam, the Hawaiian whine of phonographs slowly passing through sunshine and shade and a girl's hand gently twirling this way and that the handle of her peacock-bright parasol as she reclined on the cushions of the punt which I dreamily navigated.

On visits to Berlin and Paris during the holidays, he kept up a hectic love life, on one occasion being challenged by a hotheaded Russian stage director to a duel—which, like his father, he tactfully managed to avoid. Meanwhile the dandified Sergey became an enthusiastic devotee of Diaghilev's Russian Ballet, one of the great cultural ornaments of the Russian exile community. After Nabokov's father opened the Russian language newspaper *Rul'*, his favorite son began contributing occasional poems under the pseudonym Sirin (pronounced *See*-rin, which derives from the sirens of Greek mythology, a connection which all his life Nabokov mistakenly denied, a rare error from one who so prided himself upon his philological pedantry). The writer V. Sirin was determined not to live under the shadow of his father's famous name.

When the great Russian poet Alexander Blok died in Russia in August 1921, Nabokov and his father attended the memorial service, and Sirin recited a poetic tribute. Even at this early stage, he was already beginning to make a name for himself as a young, up-and-coming poet in Russian emigré circles. Sirin's next public appearance would be at the funeral of his father, who was to be assassinated in error a few months later. Afterward, in a daze of grief, Nabokov returned to Cambridge for his final exams in French and Russian literature. With offhand ease he obtained first-class honors, even pausing in the midst of one exam for Sirin to answer the call of the muse and jot down a poem.

After graduation, Nabokov and his brother Sergey returned to Berlin, where contacts had furnished them both with posts in a bank. The hapless Sergey managed to hold down his job for only weeks; Nabokov found that he had endured enough after just three hours. He decided that his time was better employed making a Russian translation of *Alice in Wonderland*. This was but an early example of the extracurricular work that Sirin would be forced to take on during the following lean years while he mastered his trade. Guilt at his inability to produce extra funds for his mother, who preferred eking out her existence in Prague, further contributed to his discomfort during this period. Nabokov also was forced to take on tutoring, in any one of three languages, and a few spells as a glamorous tennis coach.

As the handsome and poetically gifted son of a famous Russian father, Nabokov cut quite a figure among the Russian aristocratic diaspora, many of whom were only just beginning to feel the pinch of reduced circumstances and the German currency inflation. This glamorous aspect of Nabokov's public persona was further reinforced by his essay in *Rul'* on the joys of life in "Kambridzh." He soon became engaged to Svetlana Siewert, the seventeen-year-old daughter of a rich Russian mining engineer, and visited her regularly at the family residence on Lichterfelde, traveling there by tram. Later Nabokov would recall how, "On the Berlin-Lichterfelde streetcar [I noticed a regular fellow-passenger]. One could not forget that face, its pallor, the tightness of the skin, those most extraordinary eyes, hypnotic eyes, glowing in a cave. Years later when I first saw a photo of Kafka I recognized him immediately." These "theoretically possible glimpses of Kafka," as he called them, are an early instance of the diamond-precise whimsy that would later provide such a glittering ornament to the body of his work. V. Sirin's early attemps at prose in the form of short stories and novels in Russian were to prove somewhat less brilliant.

Understandably, his eviction from the Eden of his beloved homeland had left him artistically disorientated. V. Sirin would not only have to find his own voice, like any other novice writer, but he would be faced with the problem of finding a suitable setting for it. The latter problem was postponed in his first, heavily autobiographical novel, *Mashenka* (Mary). This features an artistic young Russian emigré called Ganin; it describes his life in exile in Berlin and his memories of his passionate love affair back in Russia with the teenage Mary. The book is permeated with the feeling of exile. Ganin is sustained by his memories of Mary, but by the end of the book he has devoured them and comes to terms with his exile: "He realized with merciless clarity that his affair with Mary was ended forever . . . he had exhausted his memories, was sated by them, and the image of Mary . . . was already a memory. Other than that image no Mary existed, nor could exist." This precipitate young judgment is given a particular poignancy by Nabokov's introduction, written over half a lifetime later, where he speaks "of nostalgia's remaining throughout one's life an insane companion, with whose heartrending oddities one is accustomed to put up in public." Even the uncharacteristic awkwardness expresses hurt.

His next novel was *King, Queen, Knave*. As Nabokov would write in his hindsightful introduction to the English translation of this work, which appeared forty years after the original: "Of all my novels, this bright brute is the gayest."

From its confident opening, the reader feels that he is in the hands of a master of his craft: "The huge black clock hand is still at rest but is on the point of making its once-a-minute gesture; that resilient jolt will set a whole world in motion." This work, in its English verison, shows much of the rich playfulness of Nabokov's mature style. Alas, this was not the case with the Russian original, where such masterly self-confidence still lay several years of resilient jolts ahead. *King, Queen, Knave* was translated "in collaboration with the author," who freely admits to "revampments of the light-hearted and highhanded order." This translation, and that of his consequent early Berlin novels, should not be mistaken for faithful renderings of the original works—in the words of one Russian-speaking observer, they are "upholstered" versions. Nabokov went to great pains to disguise what he called the "flaws, the artifacts of innocence and inexperience, which any criticule could tabulate with jocose ease." All this of course makes for better reading, and it is perhaps best to forget the original which the palimpsest obscures.

King, Queen, Knave enters the darker territory that would become increasingly characteristic of Nabokov's writing of this period. Franz arrives in Berlin and begins working for his wife's cousin, Kurt Dreyer. Kurt's wife Martha begins an affair with Franz. Eventually the two lovers decide to murder Kurt and make it look like an accident. During their holiday on the Baltic, Martha and Franz plan to push Kurt overboard from a dinghy. But just as they are about to do this, Kurt reveals that he is on the point of closing a deal that will make him $100,000, so they decide to postpone the murder. . . . There are many subtle twists to the plot, and the novel has a cinematic style, influenced by German cinema of the period. It also features German characters, though at one point an anagramatic character called Bladvak Vinomori crops up. The novel was well received in the Russian literary community, and German translation rights brought some much-needed cash. But Nabokov's hopes of the book being transformed into a lucrative film came to nothing.

So far Nabokov's work had aspired to much, yet by comparison had achieved little. In his next full-length work, *The Defense*, much is promised and much is achieved. This, without doubt, is a masterpiece. The plot of the novel is simply told, but Nabokov's telling of it brings a new depth of psychological creation to the genre. The central character is Luzhin, whom we meet as a difficult child, about to be sent away to school for the first time. Here, symbolically, he will no longer be known by his child-friendly forenames but will be addressed by his surname Luzhin. Piece by piece Nabokov assembles the mind of an exceptional but exceptionally vulnerable child. For Luzhin, the external world consists of a constant attack, against which he must try to construct a defense. At the age of eleven he discovers the ideal form of this defense in the form of chess. This is his way to transform the world from a threatening three-dimensional muddle into the precise tactics of a two-dimensional black-and-white board.

This construction of a chess genius, his motives, as well as the development and extension of his exceptional ability is utterly convincing and is told with an originality that matches the character it describes. This is Luzhin's first encounter with the game for which he has been born:

> With gnawing envy and irritating frustration Luzhin watched the game, striving to perceive those harmonious patterns the musician had spoken of and feeling vaguely that in some way or other he understood the game better than these two, although he was completely ignorant of how it should be conducted, why this was good and that was bad, and what one should do to penetrate the opposite King's camp without losses.

And here we encounter his thought processes:

> He usually went to school in a cab and always made a careful study of the cab's number, dividing it up in a special way in order the better to store it away in his memory and extract it thence whole should he require it.

In the second period of the novel, which takes place sixteen years later, Luzhin is preparing for the tournament against his great rival Turati, the winner to go forward as the challenger for the world championship. Luzhin is by now well steeped in his mental obsession with chess and capable only of awkward social intercourse. But he has at last attracted the attention of a woman who appears capable of reaching into his mentally absorbed personality and communicating with him. She understands what he is and is filled with sympathy for him. She is determined to defend him against the world that so oppresses him, and they become engaged. The end result is disastrous for Luzhin. During the tournament his concentration is distracted by his love for his new fiancée. The struggle between his immense cerebral willpower and his feelings brings on a mental breakdown.

The final part of the novel takes place the following winter, with Luzhin gradually recovering from his collapse. His fiancée, together with a well-intentioned doctor, have concluded that chess is the root of Luzhin's problem: this is what prevents him from becoming a full human being. Luzhin is briefly convinced, and once again he experiences the joy and reassurance of love. But as the clenched core of his being at last unfurls, he begins to react as only he knows how. As if his life has become a game of chess, he senses threats in every direction. He must decipher the patterns and erect a defense against them. In the end he is driven to distraction: he becomes persuaded that the only way he can defend himself against the life-chess that threatens to overwhelm him is to commit suicide. He flings himself from a bathroom window, only to notice, as he hurtles to the ground, that the flagstones of the courtyard below have become like the squares of a chessboard.

Throughout the novel we do not learn the first names that Luzhin has been forced to abandon on going to school. Only when those attempting to prevent his suicide manage to break in through the locked door to the bathroom do we hear:

"Aleksandr Ivanovich, Aleksandr Ivanovich," roared several voices.

But there was no Aleksandr Ivanovich.

The Defense is a work of considerable psychological depth, which is achieved by empathy rather than analysis—especially Freudian psychoanalysis, which Nabokov regarded as a fraud, and whose leader he was in the habit of referring to as "the Viennese Quack." Many sought to find in Luzhin a photographic negative of Nabokov himself, but he dismissed such speculation. He always insisted that his characters were purely literary creations, not to be considered outside the context in which he had created them. He could be equally dismissive of literary sleuths, though he delighted in scattering clues and counterclues for them. Concerning *The Defense*, he helpfully remarked: "For the benefit of such sleuths, I may as well confess that I gave Luzhin my French governess, my pocket chess set, and the stone of the peach I plucked in my own walled garden." Such impish jests were intended to defend him against intrusive personal prying, in much the same way as Luzhin sought to defend himself against a harsh world. Nabokov wanted the clues and references that littered his texts to direct the reader further into the book rather than beyond its covers to the author.

By now Nabokov himself had undergone a transformation. From the chrysalis of the self-confident but damaged displaced person had emerged the self-confident but nonetheless damaged butterfly of genius. In the course of this transformation we may detect, despite the obfuscation of genius, certain elements that made themselves felt in his work. Nabokov's pride had received a serious blow when his engagement to Svetlana Siewert was broken off by her rich parents, who considered a penniless tennis coach and so-called writer unsuitable for their daughter, and whisked her off to a luxurious German spa to recover from this mismatch. A few months later Nabokov met and fell in love with Vera Slonim. She was just two years younger than he, and also came from a wealthy St. Petersburg family, though her family was filled with rich Jewish merchants rather than senior political figures. Vera's life too had recently been blighted by a family tragedy, when her father left her mother to take up with a much younger cousin of his wife.

Vera was different from Nabokov's previous women friends. She was attracted as much by his literary abilities as she was by his mournful good looks. Her understanding melted the defenses of the dashing but damaged young genius. He wrote to her, "You are the one person who I can talk to—about the line of a cloud, about the singing of a thought." They were married in 1925, and Vera at once set about her lifelong task of supporting and encouraging her husband. From now on she would type out the handwritten drafts of his work, read and comment upon them, and even take on secretarial work to support them both.

Nabokov himself continued with his tennis coaching, becoming a freelance boxing instructor during the winter months. He also devised chess problems for *Rul'* and began composing the first Russian crossword puzzles—to which he gave the name *krestoslovitsa*, a word of peculiarly apt resonance, difficulty, and beauty. Alas, the name ultimately adopted by the Russian language would come from the Soviet side: the crass and corny *krossvord*. This was indicative of much that was happening to the Russian people, the Russian language, and Russian culture. In the homeland a new brash egalitarianism was emerging; meanwhile in the diaspora, all that had once been so mellifluous in the Russian ethos was becoming effete. Nabokov, for all his strengths, would not be immune from this seemingly unavoidable drift among a people cut off from their roots. As the Russian disapora dispersed from Berlin to Paris, from Europe to the Americas, the prospect of non-Soviet Russian culture becoming extinct loomed large. In 1929, the same year *The Defense* first appeared in Berlin, the great Diaghilev died, leaving his Russian Ballet facing bankruptcy, and any hope of moderation in the Soviet Union disappeared with the banishing of Trotsky and the increasing horrors of Stalin's program for agricultural collectivization.

In 1932, Nabokov wrote *Despair* (or, in Russian, *Otchayanie*—"a far more sonorous howl," as the author put it). Here Nabokov's work achieves a further depth by using a first-person narrator whose reliability we soon understand is suspect. Hermann Karlovich is a chocolate manufacturer, a German born of a Russian mother, who lives in Berlin. He claims to be a talented artist, though his chosen genre is crime. It soon becomes clear that his abilities as an artist are limited. Hermann is a murderer whose narcissistic misunderstanding of art proves at least part of his undoing. The ingenuity of this novel lies in its ever playful, ever more cunning telling. In a final ingenious move, Hermann attempts to elude arrest by trying to persuade the crowd gathered outside his house alongside the police that his escape will be just a rehearsal for a film scene. Through the open window he calls down to them:

> "A famous film actor will presently come running out of this house. He is an archcriminal but he must escape. You are asked to prevent them from grabbing him. This is part of the plot. . . . I want a clean getaway. That's all. Thank you. I'm coming out now."

When this work was translated into French, what Nabokov most feared was perceived as becoming increasingly apparent in his work. The young Jean-Paul Sartre, from whom Nabokov would later covertly borrow and then overtly disparage, perceptively remarked:

> M. Nabokov no longer believes in his [characters] or even the art of the novel. . . . I fear that M. Nabokov, like his hero, has read too much. But I see another resemblance between the author and his character. Both are victims of the war and emigration. . . . There now exists a curious literature of Russian emigrés and others who are *rootless*. The rootlessness of Nabokov . . . is total. He does not concern himself with any society, even to revolt against it, because he is not of any society.

Ironically, Nabokov's fellow emigré and friend, the celebrated poet Khodasevich, pinpointed an element of this very same tendency as Nabokov's great strength:

> The theme of Sirin's art is art itself; this is the first thing that must be said about him. . . . The urge to transfer himself into his double, to turn the reality surrounding the narrator

inside out . . . does not all of this bespeak an intricate allegory behind which is concealed not the despair of a murderer scheming for money, but the despair of an artist incapable of believing in the object of his art? This *despair* constitutes the basic motif of the best things created by Sirin. It puts him on a level with the most significant artists in contemporary European literature.

Others continued to see this as Nabokov's fatal flaw. As his art grew, so there was a tendency for it to overwhelm his subject matter. The veracity of his settings and characters threatened to become submerged in the undertow of the author's all-pervasive talent. Combined with his unavoidable rootlessness, this would become an increasing problem. How long could he go on writing about exiles in a gradually shrinking state of exiledom?

By the time *Despair* was being published in a Russian-language magazine in Paris, Hitler and the Nazis had come to power in Germany. Unlike many Russian emigrés, Nabokov chose to stay put in Berlin, partly at least because Vera's employment as a secretary provided a considerable part of their family income. Now that the world was plunged into the Great Depression, employment was scarce, and few had money to spare on private tennis coaching.

The writer Sirin was now beginning to emerge as Vladimir Nabokoff-Sirin, the name under which he published *Despair*. When the Russian emigré writer Ivan Bunin became the first Russian to receive the Nobel Prize for Literature, in 1933, Nabokov appeared on the stage beside him as the leading figure of the coming generation. But fame among such an increasingly impecunious small community did not bring financial success.

In May 1934, Vera gave birth to Nabokov's son Dmitri. In the same week an English publisher showed interest in publishing a translation of *Despair*. Nabokov at once set about the task of translating his Russian into a language he spoke but no longer felt at home in, admitting to some difficulty in the process. Thirty years later, in the introduction to the second "upholstered" translation, Nabokov boasted, "For the present edition, I have done more than revamp my thirty-year-old translation: I have revised *Otchayanie* itself." He also claimed that the entire English stock of the original English translation had been destroyed by a German bomb landing on London during World War II, "The only copy extant is, as far as I know, the one I own—but two or three may still be lurking amidst abandoned reading matter on the dark shelves of seaside boarding houses from Bournemouth to Tweedmouth." Fortunately the copy in the British Library has survived, enabling us to compare these two translations. This reveals a classic Nabokov tease—or double-tease, to be more precise. The later edition follows virtually word for word the English of the original. Page after page is *precisely* the same, and felicitously so. The English is flawless. But: in the original translation, Hermann's last thought is: "How about opening the window and making a little speech . . ." Only in the later version do the six lines of the hilarious "film rehearsal" speech appear, with its insinuated tiny suggestion that the end may not in fact be inevitable. Thus we are forced to concede that this mere six lines does "more than revamp my thirty-year-old translation" and that it does indeed confirm Nabokov's claim to "have revised *Otchayanie* itself." Escapism and great art are not incompatible.

By 1936, Hitler's campaign against the Jews was intensifying. Because she was half-Jewish, Vera was dismissed from her secretarial work. Then Nabokov learned that the Russian community was being "investigated." Worse still, the murderer of Nabokov's father, the Russian right-wing fanatic Sergey Taboritsky, had been released from prison and appointed by the Nazis to play a leading role in this investigation. Nabokov realized that he was now in real danger. In January 1937 he and Vera left to take up residence in Paris.

Meanwhile money was exceedingly short, and Nabokov began writing to anyone he could think of in search of work, anywhere. He suggested that if necessary he was even willing to work in the "wilderness" of an obscure university in America. At the same time he continued writing. He completed a novel called *Laughter in the Dark*, which is about a rich art critic called Albinus who falls inappropriately in love with Magda, a cinema usherette. In this novel the laughter is bitter and the darkness pitch black. It ends with one of Nabokov's most devilish scenes: the jealous Albinus, now blind, is silently mocked by Magda; he is unable to see that her lover has joined her and is living with them. There is no denying the novel's brilliance, but its combination of wit and bleakness succeeds only in contributing to its shallowness. Emotional life is reduced to no more than a heartless game, and the novel itself becomes little more than an intelligent entertainment.

During this early Parisian period, Nabokov also completed another highly accomplished novel, *The Gift*. This recounts at some length and complexity the artistic development of a writer in 1920s Berlin. It includes much subtle parody, perverse but precise observation, and humorous fooling with the reader. Although Nabokov's art remained as resilient as ever, there

49

was no doubt that it was turning in on itself. This becomes clear from the opening sentence:

> One cloudy but luminous day, towards four in the afternoon on April the first, 192—(a foreign critic once remarked that while many novels, most German ones for example, begin with a date, it is only Russian authors who, in keeping with the honesty peculiar to our literature, omit the final digit), a moving van, very long and very yellow, hitched to a tractor that was also yellow, the hypertrophied rear wheels and a shamelessly exposed anatomy, pulled up in front of Number Seven Tannenberg Street, in the west part of Berlin.

In Paris the Nabokovs lived in what Nabokov would later call "semi-poverty." It was a life devoid of luxuries but nonetheless included cheap holidays and lively literary gatherings among similarly penniless intellectuals. In this way Nabokov met James Joyce (who asked about the Russian recipe for mead) and the passionate Russian poet Marina Tsvetaeva (who compiled with him a list of the writers they most disliked).

Even after his marriage, Nabokov had not been above the odd infidelity when the occasion arose. But these were merely casual attachments, easily dispensed with. Now, in a comeuppance that may well account for the emotional tone of *Laughter in the Dark*, Nabokov found himself falling deeply in love with a Russian emigré divorcee called Irina Guadinini. For once, reality outdid Nabokov: Irina was not a cinema usherette but a poodle groomer. Nabokov eventually became so distraught that he confessed the affair to Vera when the family were staying in the south of France. Had Vera not proved so intransigent, the affair would probably have broken up their marriage. As it was, Nabokov stayed with Vera and their three-year-old son Dmitri, and wrote asking Irina to return his passionate love letters to her, "which anyway, have much writer's exaggeration in them."

In his work Nabokov may frequently have mocked emotional naiveté and intensity, but the fact that he himself had experienced such excruciating feelings, and made a fool of himself in a similar fashion, seems to have lent his descriptions a surreptitious poignancy. His descriptions are not *quite* heartless and often contain a tantalizing irony. He is painfully aware of what he is describing. It comes as only a slight surprise that in his younger, more poetic days, Nabokov wrote enthusiastically about the passionate novels of Dostoevsky (whom he later dismissed contemptuously). Even during this more mature period, he did claim to see the artistry in the raw, almost hysterical power of Tsvetaeva's poetry, though at the same time maintaining that he could never have written this way himself (except, pehaps, in letters that are now destroyed).

In Nabokov's next novel, *The Real Life of Sebastian Knight*, there is a telling scene in which Sebastian Knight's half-brother, known only as V throughout the novel, comes across two bundles of letters written to the deceased writer Sebastian Knight. V decides to follow his dead half-brother's instructions and destroy the letters unread. From the handwriting he recognizes that one bundle contains letters from Clare Bishop, Sebastian's faithful companion, who read his books, edited them, and even advised him on them. Only as the flames are reducing the other bundle to a cinder does he notice that these letters are from a woman writing in Russian. During the ensuing months V begins to realize how important these Russian letters were. The only way he will ever understand Sebastian Knight's true nature will be if he can find out who this Russian woman was.

The Real Life of Sebastian Knight is about V's attempt to discover the "real life" of his half-brother, whom he has not known properly since they were young emigrants from Russia. In order to write this biography of his half-brother, V must abandon writing in his native Russian and turn to English. This "biography-novel" by V is filled with many a literary sleight of hand, as well as all kinds of false scents and deceptions— to the point where it becomes possible that the book is in fact not a fictional biography at all but a fictional autobiography written by Sebastian Knight himself. It ends on a tantalizing note, as if the whole book has been nothing but a play performed by actors:

> . . . the masquerade draws to a close. The bald little prompter shuts his book, as the light fades gently. The end, the end. They all go back to their everyday life . . . but the hero remains, for, try as I may, I cannot get out of my part: Sebastian's mask clings to my face, the likeness will not be washed off. I am Sebastian, or Sebastian is I, or perhaps we are both someone whom neither of us knows.

Despite all the book's accomplished artistry and cleverness, it was apparent that once again Nabokov's subject matter was turning dangerously in upon itself. Yet here there was one saving grace, one element that Nabokov could not entirely manipulate. Nabokov knew that his future now lay elsewhere than as a Russian-language emigré writer in Berlin. And now that he was in Paris, he decided that he had no future as a Russian-language emigré writer at all. Instead he bravely determined that from now on he would write in English. *The Real Life of Sebast-*

ian Knight was the first novel that he wrote directly in English. Sebastian Knight's abandonment of his Russian lover may have had personal emotional echoes in the author's life, but it also had strong metaphorical literary echoes. In the novel, Nabokov was abandoning his beloved Russian heritage, the language to which he had been born, for a future as an unknown English-language writer. Like a Russian doll, the novel opens to reveal inner facsimile after inner facsimile, the deeper one looks.

While Nabokov was writing *The Real Life of Sebastian Knight*, he also suffered another decisive break with his Russian past. By 1938 his aging mother was becoming increasingly ill in Prague. Nabokov's semi-poverty was such that he could not send her anything or even travel to see her. He desperately tried to borrow money so that she could obtain better medical treatment, but to little avail. Then suddenly things took a turn for the worse. It became evident that his mother was dying, and in March 1938 the Germans marched into Czechoslovakia. Nabokov realized that his last chance to see his mother had now passed: he would have been arrested as soon as he set foot in Nazi territory. Two months later his mother died.

Europe was now on the brink of war, yet Nabokov remained astonishingly unaware of the seriousness of the political situation. He boasted that he seldom read the newspapers, and this appears to have been true. In his view, the writer had no business whatsoever involving himself in politics. Still, he continued trying to obtain an academic post in the United States—mainly because he had now chosen to write in English, and this was where his main readership would be. By now, however, several English and American publishers had already turned down *The Real Life of Sebastian Knight*. The message seemed to be that he may have mastered the English language but not the way English-speaking people wrote literature.

In September 1939, Hitler invaded Poland, with the result that Britain and France declared war on Germany, signaling the start of World War II in Europe. A month later, Nabokov embarked upon what appeared to be a retrograde move. He began a short novella in Russian called *Volsheb-nik* (The Enchanter). This features a middle-aged man with a penchant for young girls, who marries a sickly woman in order to gain access to her twelve-year-old daughter. When the mother dies, he takes the daughter on holiday. He enters her bed, but the daughter wakes up and begins screaming hysterically. In fright, he rushes out of the hotel into the street, where he is run over by the "growing, grinning, megathundering mass" of a lorry: "Zigzag gymnastics of lightning, spectrogram of a thunderbolt's split seconds—and the film of life had burst."

Despite such literary pyrotechnics, the novella as a whole didn't seem to work, and Nabokov put it aside. In May 1940 the Germans invaded France. Nabokov and his family fled Paris and managed to obtain a berth on the *Champlain*, which sailed from St. Nazaire for America, the last passenger liner to leave France before it was overrun by the Germans.

Nabokov seems to have decided in advance that he would like America. As a result, his first impressions were hugely, almost naively positive. Not for him the elitist European approach which regarded America as brash and its inhabitants as boorish philistines. On the contrary, here was a delight, an entire new world filled with largely undreamt of wonders, for him to explore and admire. What was opening up before him was a fresh, unignorable reality. Unlike the history-steeped backdrop to his European life, this could not be manipulated at will or used to provide mirroring literary reflections for the sophisticated observer. Here was a world that demanded to be seen on its own terms.

From the start, Nabokov did his best to avoid emigré Russian groups, whose members had a tendency to be snobbish and anti-Semitic. But he did contact the Tolstoy Foundation, which had been set up to assist Russian immigrants to America. The foundation promised to seek out suitable employment for him, and a job was soon arranged at Scribner's Bookstore, on Fifth Avenue in New York City, as a bicycle delivery boy. The forty-one-year-old Nabokov politely turned down the offer. During the winter of 1940 he supported himself with occasional private tutoring and obtained a temporary job classifying butterflies at the Museum of Natural History in New York. He enjoyed this return to his beloved hobby, and though the pay was negligible, the post usefully established his presence in lepidopterist circles.

Early in 1941, Nabokov obtained a temporary post teaching creative writing at Stanford University in California. A woman he had tutored drove Nabokov and his family across America. Here he encountered for the first time American motels and the broadly different customs of American life, and caught his first glimpses of the vast, fluttering variety of American butterflies in the wild. Holidays and trips in Europe had for the most part meant a return to resorts such as he had known since his privileged childhood. On his travels in America, Nabokov confronted an utterly new world and responded with childish delight. The students who attended his summer classes at Stanford regarded the stooping, stick-thin Russian in old tennis shoes as an awesome European genius, the like of which they had never previously encountered. Nabokov read them passages from *The Real Life of Sebastian Knight*, dutifully explaining the interplay of reality and illusion in the text.

On his return to the East Coast, Nabokov obtained a temporary teaching position at Wellesley College and another part-time position at the nearby Entomological Department of the Harvard Museum, before finally being offered a permanent post at Wellesley. At this prestigous women's college, Nabokov lectured on modern European literature. Here, among groups of admiring young American women, he was in his element. This was the era when well-brought-up young American women wore sweaters, plaid skirts, and bobby socks; the seven years that Nabokov remained at Wellesley were punctuated by a series of surreptitious hand-holding crushes, though no serious infidelities. The naive European philanderer had fallen amidst emotionally manipulative young American women who knew perfectly well how to handle such a flattering old admirer.

Things were also progressing with Nabokov's literary career. In his early search for work, he had been recommended to call on Edmund Wilson, the best-known American literary critic of the time. Wilson managed to secure several book review assignments for Nabokov and was highly impressed with the erudite pieces he produced. When *The Real Life of Sebastian Knight* was finally accepted by an American publisher, Wilson read the manuscript and found it "absolutely enchanting." He wrote to Nabokov, "It's amazing that you should write such fine English prose and not sound like any other English writer." It so happened that Wilson had just learned Russian for his book on Russian thinkers, *To the Finland Station*, and he soon became a close friend of Nabokov, exchanging views on Russian and European literature.

Nabokov now began trying out his English on short stories, a form in which his impish delight (or perversity) had always flourished. Owing to the success of his lectures on modern European literature, especially those on the great Russian writers, Nabokov was commissioned to write a book on Gogol, one of his favorite authors. The publisher had in mind a brief critical work for students; Nabokov thought otherwise and began composing a book which he originally entitled *Gogol Through the Looking Glass*, a reference to the sequel of *Alice in Wonderland*. He had a subject, so the work was never in danger of becoming entirely self-referential; yet it certainly displayed many of Nabokov's more abstruse literary talents, being by turns willful and playful. Contrary to expectation, Gogol's birth appears at the very end of the book, which instead opens boldly with the announcement:

> Nikolai Gogol, the strangest prose-poet Russia ever produced, died Thursday morning, a little before eight, on the fourth of March, eighteen fifty-two, in Moscow. He was almost forty-three years old—a reasonably ripe age for him, considering the ridiculously short span of life generally allotted to other great Russian writers of his miraculous generation.

Having begun as he meant to go on, Nabokov continued on his wayward way, ignoring such pedantic requirements as resumé or chronology, selecting his own favorite bits from various works and expounding at length upon them. As the baffled publisher wrote to Nabokov on receipt of the manuscript: "I do think the student ought to be told what it is all about." Nabokov insisted otherwise. The book is crammed with oblique observations, such as on the "strangeness" of St. Petersburg: "The chief town in Russia had been built by a tyrant of genius upon a swamp, and upon the bones of slaves rotting in that swamp; this was the root of that strangeness—and the initial flaw." The innocent student reader is regaled with references to English rugby, the logic of Lewis Carroll, the fact that the Russian word *poshlust* has no equivalent in English, French, or German, and the difference between human ocular vision and "the image perceived by the faceted eye of an insect." Approaching his supposed subject (Gogol) by a roundabout route, Nabokov also finds time to express his passing opinions on the critical faculties of the tsars ("immune to authentic literature as all rulers are"), non-Euclidian geometry ("If parallel lines do not meet it is not because they cannot, but because they have other things to do"), and even the behavior of Russia's greatest poet, who would die in a duel over his wife:

> Pushkin had just married and had brought his young wife from Moscow to the capital—instead of locking her up in the darkest closet of a remote country house as he ought to have done had he known what would come of those ridiculous court-balls and hobnobbing with knavish courtiers (under the supervision of a bland, philandering Tsar, an ignormaus and a cad, whose whole reign was not worth a single foot of Pushkin's verse).

The chapter that is allegedly about Gogol's greatest work, *The Government Inspector*, is punnily entitled, "The Government Spectre," and includes the supreme critical observation: "The plot of *The Government Inspector* is as unimportant as the plots of all Gogol's books." Nabokov was also mindful that his American readers would encounter Gogol's work in translation, and explained helpfully:

> I sometimes think that these old English "translations" are remarkably similar to the

so-called Thousand Pieces Execution which was popular at one time in China. The idea was to cut out from the patient's body one tiny square bit the size of a cough lozenge, say, every five minutes or so until bit by bit (all of them selected with discrimination so as to have the patient live to the nine hundred and ninety-ninth piece) his whole body was delicately removed.

There is no doubt that Nabokov's *Gogol* is a magical masterpiece. But it cannot in all seriousness be described as either a work of criticism devoted to Gogol or a brief biography of the Russian writer, the categories into which its publisher had forlornly hoped it might fall. To describe it as a work of fiction would certainly outrage its author, who would rightly insist upon the unimpeachable veracity of all the information it provides. There is no doubt, however, that despite its mock-pedantic solemnity, its brilliant and outrageous critical observations are often presented in the manner of comic fiction. As for instance in this passage, where Nabokov demonstrates the bizarrerie of Gogol's astounding literary technique:

> The peripheral characters of his novel are engendered by the subordinate clauses of its various metaphors, comparisons, and lyrical outbursts. We are faced by the remarkable phenomenon of mere forms of speech directly giving rise to live creatures. This is perhaps the most typical example of how this happens.
>
> "Even the weather had obligingly accommodated itself to the setting: the day was neither bright nor gloomy but of a kind of bluey-grey tint such as is found only upon the worn-out uniforms of garrison soldiers, for the rest a peaceful class of warriors except for their being somewhat inebriate on Sundays."

He goes on to say how difficult it is to convey in English the "curves of this life-generating syntax" which succeed in forming a bridge between "a dim landscape under a dull sky and a groggy old soldier accosting the reader with a rich hiccup on the festive outskirts of the very same sentence."

Any readers willing to enter through Nabokov's looking glass will find this book the most amusing and illuminating work on various apects of Gogoliana they are ever likely to encounter. Even so, they will also be aware that the book says just as much about the sensibilities of its author as it does about its subject. Fortunately Nabokov's publisher saw the joke, and the book was issued. It was greeted by the critics with cautious bafflement, sold few copies, and remains an all-but-forgotten masterpiece. Unlikely as it may seem, this book would prove to be a mere trial run for Nabokov's most serious and heartfelt piece of critical literature. *Gogol* was no passing work of flimsy whimsy; this was a rehearsal for the flight of one of the most amazing butterflies ever to be seen in the critical firmament, his controversial Pushkin translation. Already Nabokov had conceived of the idea of translating Pushkin's masterpiece, the greatest poem in Russian literature, suggesting to Edmund Wilson: "Why don't we write together a scholarly prose translation of *Evgenii Onegin* with copious notes?" But for the time being nothing came of this project.

Both before and after writing *Gogol*, Nabokov attempted another dress rehearsal. Before *Gogol* he had begun tinkering with his abandoned Russian novella *The Enchanter*, turning it into English. After finishing *Gogol*, he began transforming this work into a full-scale novel, set in America, about a middle-aged man and a twelve-year-old girl with the Spanish-sounding name of Juanita Darc (a pun on Joan of Arc). But as he progressed he found himself increasingly "beset with technical difficulties and doubts." In a fit of despair he abandoned the novel and this time decided to destroy it, along with his copious accumulated notes on the subject (especially the details of Americana that he had meticulously noted on stacks of index cards during his travels and holidays). Fortunately, as he was carrying all the papers to the garden incinerator, Vera demanded to know what he was doing, and then forcefully dissuaded him from burning so much as a single index card.

Nabokov later conceded that had his wife not intervened so decisively, "the ghost of my destroyed book would have haunted my files for the rest of my life."

With the ending of World War II in 1945, news began reaching America of the horrors of Nazism. Nabokov had assumed that his brother Sergey had taken refuge in the castle of his Austrian lover. But this had not been the case. In 1943, Sergey had been arrested by the Nazis as a homosexual and had perished in a concentration camp outside Hamburg. For years Nabokov had clung to his Nansen passport (issued to stateless persons between the world wars), thus avoiding the need to commit himself to any European nation in which he resided. In light of his brother's death, it comes as little surprise that Nabokov now chose to commit himself to America and become an American citizen.

His appearance changed around this time, transforming him from the tall lean figure of his youth to the plump avuncular man of his more mature years. Nabokov had always been a heavy smoker, and in 1945 he began to suffer from heart palpitations. His doctor advised him to give up smoking, which he managed by a supreme effort of will aided by the compulsive consumption of molasses candy, which caused him to put on a great many pounds in just a few months. Wherever he went, he carried with him a paper bag of "molasses kisses," even consuming them during his lectures. (Nabokov had previously smoked while delivering his lectures, a practice which was not unknown at the time.)

After seven years at Wellesley, Nabokov was appointed professor of Russian literature at Cornell. Here he continued to deliver nonsmoking lectures, honing his ideas on Pushkin's *Onegin* and over the years expanding his course to include the masterpieces of European fiction. Nabokov was a curious lecturer, by turns wayward, endearing, and pedantic. As with his work on Gogol, it was difficult to realize that he was being serious, and what exactly he was being serious about. He did not wish to turn his students into third-rate literary critics, a calling for which they were ill-suited and which almost none of them would end up practicing. Instead it was his aim to turn them into "major readers of major writers." He was not interested in the symbolism or social context of the works he discussed, nor any other such orthodox and pedestrian matters. As he blithely commented on Joyce: "*Ulysses*, of course, is a divine work of art and will live on despite the academic nonentities who turn it into a collection of symbols or Greek myths." The fact that its overall structure was based upon the travels of Homer's Ulysses, and that its plot contained countless symbolic echoes and references to his epic voyage, was dismissed as irrelevant. Other great writers were likely to be dismissed out hand. Dostoevsky, for instance, was characterized as "a mediocre writer" whose work consisted for the most part of "wastelands of literary platitudes." He complained that so many "do not know the difference between real literature and pseudo-literature, and to such readers Dostoevski may seem more important and more artistic than such trash as our American historical novels or things called *From Here to Eternity* and such like balberdash." (Note the inclusive use of the word "our," with which this new

American cunningly sought to absolve himself from any such crass charge as European snobbery or anti-Americanism.)

What Nabokov wished to convey was the role of the writer as an "enchanter." As he constantly insisted, all great literature is "a fairy tale." His biographer Brian Boyd perceptively points out: "He treats novels . . . as little worlds, about which we can and should find out more and more." In the course of his lectures Nabokov would draw maps, sketches of the places in which a novel is set, even the layout of rooms in which the action takes place. Detail was what interested him, the detail that brought to life the world it described, the hint of a triumphant smile that revealed what was really taking place between two characters, and of course detail for its own perverse Nabokovian sake. Discussing Kafka's *Metamorphosis*, in which the hero Gregor Samsa is turned into a "monstrous insect," Nabokov asks:

> Now what exactly is the "vermin" into which poor Gregor, the seedy commercial traveller,

is so suddenly transformed? It obviously belongs to the branch of "jointed leggers" (*Arthropoda*), to which insects, and spiders, and centipedes, and crustaceans belong. If the "numerous little legs" mentioned in the beginning mean more than six legs, then Gregor would not be an insect from a zoological point of view. But I suggest that a man awakening on his back and finding he has as many as six legs vibrating in the air might feel that six was sufficient to be called numerous. We shall therefore assume that Gregor has six legs, that he is an insect.

The lecturer then proceeds to ask what kind of insect this could be—remarking that some commentators insist that it is a cockroach, "which of course does not make sense." And so on. . . .

Nabokov's examinations could be even more detailed, with searching questions such as: "Who is 'the man in the brown mackintosh' in Joyce's *Ulysses*?" (Nabokov had developed his own theory that this mysterious character, who appears fleetingly and peripherally in just a few scenes of this lengthy book, was in fact Joyce himself "observing his own work." No other critics concur in this conjecture, but heaven help the poor student who had the temerity to question the master's pet thesis. Those who played the game were well rewarded with lenient marking; those who did not, or who made unwary remarks suggesting that Dostoevsky was a great writer, were liable to be imperiously flunked.) Other favorite exam questions included the chestnut: "What kind of insect did Gregor Samsa turn into?" and, most notoriously of all, "Discuss Flaubert's use of the word 'and.'" This latter caused such a furor among students and staff that it prompted calls for Nabokov's dismissal—which he only narrowly averted by maintaining that this serious question went to the very heart of Flaubert's writing, defying anyone to contradict his meticulously argued thesis.

These idiosyncratic standards were no pose. Indeed, they were the very principles that governed Nabokov's own creative output, with which he continued throughout his teaching career. In between his lectures on literary etymology and entomology, Nabokov once again turned to the nearly burnt mansucript about the middle-aged man and the twelve-year-old girl. This time she had a new name:

> Lolita, light of my life, fire of my loins. My sin, my soul. Lo-lee-ta: the tip of the tongue taking a trip of three steps down the palate to tap, at three, on the teeth. Lo. Lee. Ta.
>
> She was Lo, plain Lo, in the morning, standing four feet ten in one sock. She was Lola in slacks. She was Dolly at school. She was Dolores on the dotted line. But in my arms she was always Lolita.

This is demonstrably the most lyrical opening to a novel in all modern fiction. There is no mistaking the ecstasy of love. Here, if ever proof were needed, is an example of the great writer as enchanter. But there is also no denying that this is the rapture of a middle-aged man, Humbert Humbert, for the pre-teenage girl who became his stepdaughter—the same man who also callously shot his rival lover. As Humbert Humbert himself comments, "You can always count on a murderer for a fancy prose style."

Pedophilia and cold-blooded murder are hardly guaranteed to endear the reader, and those who commit such crimes cannot easily enchant us with the loving memories of their misdeeds. Yet Humbert Humbert is no Ancient Mariner buttonholing his listener with a poetic account of his seagull-inspired misfortunes. On the contrary, Humbert's occasional halfhearted regrets ("these miserable memories") are far outweighed by his heartfelt raptures over these same memories ("treasures"). And we find ourselves regaled rather than repelled—despite his teasing, mock-stern admonitions ("Human beings attend"). What are we to make of this complicity in the forbidden? Our complicity, as readers, our willing suspension—not of disbelief but of all moral sense? According to Nabokov's enlightened opinion, "A work of art cannot be obscene." Montaigne, at the outset of Enlightenment thinking, adhered to the classical maxim: "Nothing human is alien to me." Yet instead of merely casting aside our alienation, Nabokov's

Humbert surreptitiously encourages us to revel in his humanity, or at least his form of it. Reading *Lolita* is a highly enjoyable experience, even as it is an aesthetic one. Our wonderment at the sheer literary skill, and what it describes, are one and inseparable—which is far from the case with commonplace gymnastic pornography. It is worth bearing all this in mind as one wanders in delight down the primrose path of Nabokov's pedophiliac prose.

Humbert's European years, before he came to America and encountered Lolita, bear only fleeting resemblances to those of his creator, except in his skilled and playful literary tone. Humbert's voice had taken many years to achieve its full, insinuating sonority. This was a lush growth, sprouting out of the rich aesthetic earth of Nabokov's early Russian poetry, nurtured into the first longing memories of exile in Berlin, flowering in the errant genius of *The Gift*, and spreading its heartless petals in *Laughter in the Dark*. *Lolita* was a culmination, and Nabokov knew it. Hence his despair when at first he could not realize it in all the glory he knew it was capable of achieving.

Here he is a master in complete control of his material, yet his material includes America itself: a young American nymphet and the entire country of his travels. They do not bend to his will: his amazing talents had met their amazing match. Nabokov's exotic imagination was forced to coexist with an overwhelming normality. This metaphorical resonance is there in Humbert Humbert's most literal feelings:

> . . . my existence proved monstrously two-fold. Overtly, I had so-called normal relationships with a number of terrestial women having pumpkins or pears for breasts; inly, I was consumed by a hell furnace of localized lust for every passing nymphet whom as a law-abiding poltroon I never dared approach.

Humbert is already middle-aged, with a failed French marriage behind him, by the time he reaches America. Soon after his arrival, he joins an expedition to Arctic Canada, where he is resident psychiatrist. After twenty months in the frigid tundra he plans to spend the summer in

New England writing up his notes. Here he ends up boarding with the widowed Charlotte Haze:

> I think I better describe her right away, to get it over with. The poor lady was in her middle thirties, she had a shiny forehead, plucked eyebrows. . . . She was obviously one of those women whose polished words may reflect a book club or bridge club, or any other deadly conventionality, but never her soul. [She engaged in] conversations, through the sunny celophane of which not very appetizing frustrations can be readily distinguished.

Humbert discovers that Charlotte has a daughter called Lolita, and soon falls under the spell of his "hot downy darling." He begins keeping a diary, in which he records his observations of Lolita and his growing feelings for her. On one occasion she enters his room:

> As she bent her brown curls over the desk at which I was writing, Humbert the Hoarse put his arm around her in a miserable imitation of blood-relationship. . . . Her adorable profile,

parted lips, warm hair were some three inches from my bared eyetooth; and I felt the heat of her limbs through her rough tomboy clothes. All at once I knew I could kiss her throat or the wick of her mouth with perfect impunity.

We have already been made aware of Humbert's penchant for nymphets, but this only reaches its apotheosis with Lolita.

My only grudge against nature was that I could not turn my Lolita inside out and apply voracious lips to her young matrix, her unknown heart, her nacreous liver, the seagrapes of her lungs, her comely twin kidneys.

The suggestive comedy—both perverse and teasing—of this description aptly engages the reality of both Humbert's feelings and our complicity in what is going on, in what we are reading about and in our own way participating in. This weird humor is a mirror: "Human beings attend."

Humbert also records in his diary his distaste for Lolita's mother, "that Haze woman."

But Charlotte Haze becomes infatuated with Humbert, finally revealing her feelings for him in a letter:

> I am a passionate and lonely woman and you are the love of my life. Now, my dearest, *mon cher, cher monsieur*, you have read this; now you know. So, will you please, *at once*, pack and leave.

As she had hoped, Humbert stays, and they get married. But one day Dolores discovers Humbert's diary, and the truth of his feelings for her as well as his real feelings for her daughter. Mortified, she confronts Humbert: "Her face, disfigured by her emotions, was not a pretty sight." In a frenzy of anguish she eventually runs from the house and is accidentally run over. The sheer skill and calculated deftness with which Nabokov describes these scenes as Humbert recalls them is utterly convincing. The reader is made aware, simultaneously, of the tragedy of what is taking place and its banality in Humbert's cold eyes. As Humbert is remembering these scenes, he is mindful throughout of the wondrous gift that fate has placed in his lap. He is now free to take over Lolita, all for himself.

Humbert's testimony takes the form of evidence which he is giving to an imaginary court, whose task it is to judge him. As he appeals to the court, cajoles it, even attempts to endear himself to it, we become aware that *we* are the court. Although we are meant to be judging him, we are in fact carried along by his evidence. Nabokov's playful prose so enchants the reader that he is forced to understand that he too is in some obscure way guilty. He is human, just as Humbert is human. Once again we are made aware of Montaigne's wish to understand all of which human beings are capable. But Nabokov goes further than Montaigne: his prose ensures that there is little effort involved in overcoming this alien aspect of humanity. We are made more than aware of the sheer joy of Humbert's feelings. We can see and feel their innocent source: in the innocent pre-pubescent years we have all experienced. And the way Nabokov evokes it, these feelings are not confined to males. He explicitly alludes to this, with passing references to juvenile lesbiansim. Nabokov is evoking the early awakenings of sexual feeling before they are explicity directed at the opposite sex. The horror lies in the fact that Humbert is a middle-aged man who retains the sexual orientation of a twelve-year-old boy. Nabokov cunningly plays on our awakened memory of such early feelings.

In another, lamentably convincing scene, Humbert directly addresses his imaginary court as he analyzes how he and Lolita became lovers: "Did I deprive her of her flower? Sensitive gentlewomen of the jury, I was not even her first lover." In a combination of lame defense and acute insight he declares:

> I am trying to describe these things not to re-live them in my present boundless misery, but to sort out the portion of hell and the portion of heaven in that strange, awful, maddening world—nymphet love.

The origins of Humbert's feelings may have been innocent enough, and their persistence monstrous; but the object of these affections is not innocent herself, as we have seen. She also has her own peculiar juvenile mores, which shock the aged sophisticated Humbert. For example:

> It was very curious the way she considered— and kept doing so for a long time—all caresses except kisses on the mouth or the stark act of love either "romantic slosh" or "abnormal."

In may ways it is Humbert who is naive. He has entered the knowing yet innocent world of the American pre-teen. There are many such ironies, as well as a plot filled with twists and tricks, before the final, almost touching valediction from Humbert, with which he finishes his testament: "And this is the only immortality you and I may share, my Lolita."

Understandably, Nabokov could find no American publisher for *Lolita*. The book was eventually published by Maurice Girodias of the Olympia Press in Paris. Girodias used the Olympia Press to publish in English straight pornography as well as a few risqué literary works by authors such as Henry Miller, J. P. Donleavy, and Samuel Beckett, which were touted to American tourists in Paris during the summer season. Inevitably the fastidious Nabokov soon fell out with Girodias, who proved a tardy and reluctant payer; but he had served his purpose. Although *Lolita* was later banned by even the French authorities, it was at least "out," and American publishers began to show an interest. In 1958 *Lolita* was published in America by Putnam. Its appearance caused the expected furor, but it was defended by many leading literary figures as well as supported by an avid reading public. Nabokov had at last made a name for himself in America, achieving the fame and fortune he had long felt to be his due. In the ensuing years he would be recognized as one of the leading writers of the twentieth century. It had taken a sensational recalcitrant subject—an essentially artless heroine—to inspire Nabokov's fastidious art to its finest flight.

By now Nabokov had completed two further works—his painstaking translation and annotation of Pushkin's *Eugene Onegin*, and a novel called *Pnin*. The latter recounts the comic misunderstandings of an absentminded and mildly eccentric Russian emigré academic as he attempts to fit into the American university scene. It opens with a description of Pnin on a train to Cremona, but we soon learn that "Professor Pnin was on the wrong train." Many of the quirks displayed by Pnin are in fact Nabokov's own, but the skilled and crafty telling of the tale make a truly independent creation of Pnin. Even so, this is much how Nabokov had been during his early American years, and how he might have ended up if he had not achieved fame as a writer. The book concludes on a circular note, with a reference to "the story of Pnin rising to address the Cremona Women's Club and discovering he had brought the wrong lecture."

Pnin was to be Nabokov's last important work of fiction completed in America. In 1959 he gave his last lecture at Cornell and set sail for Europe, where he was to live in Switzerland. Worldwide sales of *Lolita* had made him a rich man, and together with his wife Vera he occupied the top floor of the Palace Hotel at Montreux, overlooking Lake Geneva. (This apartment had previously been the home of the Russian entertainer Peter Ustinov.) At last, forty years after being deprived of his fortune and inherited estates, Nabokov was able to live the life of *richesse* which had been his expectation, his meals prepared by chefs, with liveried servants attending to his every need.

Here Nabokov continued to put the finishing touches to his translation of *Eugene Onegin* and was visited by Edmund Wilson, with whom he had originally planned to translate this work as a joint project. In the summer of 1960 Nabokov made a screenplay of *Lolita* for the director Stanley Kubrick, who would eventually turn this into a film, with James Mason adding his own, peculiarly English blend of dark sarcasm to the role of Humbert Humbert.

Nabokov now settled down to write what would become his second consummate masterpiece, *Pale Fire*. On the surface this would appear to be Nabokov's most complex work, consisting as it does of "a poem in heroic couplets, of nine hundred and ninety-nine lines," followed by a commentary and index covering almost six times as many pages. This presents a problem for those who might wish to read the book in orthodox novelistic fashion, from start to finish. The way to read this book is to start into the poem and to refer to the copious notes at the back as one continues. These begin with a note relating to lines 1 to 4, which is over a page long. (As the Foreword so helpfully puts it, the best way to approach *Pale Fire* is by "simply purchasing two copies of the same work which can be placed in adjacent positions on a comfortable table." The difficulties attendant upon reading *Pale Fire* are purely functional and superficial: once into the book you will find that the reading of it gives as much a pure joy as it must have given Nabokov writing it.

The central poem in the book, which is itself called "Pale Fire," was composed by the well-known poet John Shade during the last twenty days of his life in July 1959, at his house in New Wye, Appalachia, U.S.A. After Shade's death, his neighbor Charles Kinbote manages to persuade his grief-stricken wife to give him the manuscript of the poem and sign over to him all editorial control over its publication. It quickly emerges that Charles Kinbote is both ruthless in his ambitions and more or less deranged. Precisely how deranged is left to the reader to judge. We learn that Kinbote is a homosexual who hero-worshiped Shade and was constantly pestering him. Kinbote has convinced himself that Shade's poem "Pale Fire" is in fact all about Kinbote himself and what Kinbote believes to have been his earlier life as King of Zembla.

Zembla is just one of the resonant and deceptive names in *Pale Fire* (the novel). New Wye, for instance, has echoes of "New Y," or New York State, the location of Cornell, where Nabokov had previously taught. The campus in which Shade and Kinbote live as neighbors bears a strong physical resemblance to Cornell. Zembla also has its particular resemblances: Novaya Zemlya is the name of the large island off the northern Arctic coast of Russia. The Zembla of Kinbote's memory (or fantasy) is a fond fabled blend of Russia and Ruritania, where Kinbote was formerly King Charles the Beloved but was deposed by a revolution. Kinbote describes, in a suitably fantastic and whimsical manner, his adventures during his escape from Zembla after the revolution. But this fantasy becomes subtly undermined by a threatening reality—which has its resonances in both the life of John Shade and the life of Nabokov's father. After the flight of Charles the Beloved, the new Zemblan authorities dispatch an assassin called Gradus to kill him. As we progress through the poem and its commentary, we learn of the gradual approach of Gradus to New Wye on his mission of death.

While Shade was writing his poem, Kinbote would frequently drop in on his neighbor and reminisce about his experiences in Zembla. Kinbote becomes convinced that the poem is filled with hidden references to Zembla and the exploits of Charles the Beloved. Needless to say, the poem has no such explicit references—though Kinbote ingeniously succeeds in detecting many covert ones, which he explains at length in his commentary. At times he even dispenses with any attempt at uncovering such supposed references and simply tells his own story. Kinbote's rampant egoism, his unbridled homosexual appetites, and his royal disdain for common life

make him a hilarious, if wrongheaded, guide to
Shade's poem.

The poem itself is by turns pedestrian (echo-
ing the approaching footsteps of the flat-footed
assassin Gradus) and Byronic in its ingenuity (if
not its inspiration):

> A preterist: one who collects cold nests.
> Here was my bedroom, now reserved for
> guests.

On some occasions, the poem has references
which resonate far beyond the ken of its author or
even its ingenious and indefatigable commentator:

> It was a year of Tempests: Hurricane
> Lolita swept from Florida to Maine.

This elicits the following note from Kinbote:

> Line 680: Lolita
> Major hurricanes are given feminine names
> in America. The feminine gender is suggested
> not so much by the sex of furies and harri-
> dans as by a general professional application.
> . . . Why our poet chose to give his 1958

hurricane a little-used Spanish name (sometimes given to parrots) instead of Linda or Lois, is not clear.

This in-joke has its own further resonances, which extend from Nabokov directly to the reader, eluding any novelistic characters in between (a favorite endearing tease). Nineteen fifty-eight was of course also the year in which *Lolita* first appeared in the United States. Its hurricane sales accounted for 100,000 copies in the first three weeks. Most of these took place along the eastern seaboard, though mainly in New York, Phildelphia, Boston, and Washington rather than strictly "from Florida to Maine." And what was the only American novel whose sales exceeded this? Needless to say, *Gone with the Wind*. (And doubtless there are other little nudges that escape this author.)

Kinbote's index at the back of the book gives further information, ranging from "*A., Baron*, Oswin Affepin, last Baron of Aff, a puny traitor, *286*" to "*Zembla*, a distant northern land." Seldom can an index have presented such a flight of poetic pedantry. It is the last thing one comes to, yet it also refers the reader back to many pages of the text, with several references that defy one not to be intrigued. Thus Nabokov not only manages to persuade the reader that he is better off buying two copies of the book, but leads him back into reading the book more than once. This is all carefully set down by Kinbote in his Foreword:

> Although those notes, in conformity with custom, come after the poem, the reader is advised to consult them first and then study the poem with their help, rereading them of course as he goes through the text, and perhaps, after having done with the poem, consulting them a third time so as to complete the picture.

It is difficult to exaggerate the delightful teasing, cunning sleights of hand, and sheer joy one experiences in reading *Pale Fire*. So is this anything more than a huge and highly amusing pedantic poetic hoax, no more than a zemblance of a serious literary work? The concentration required to remain immersed, and at the same time switch from poem to notes and back again, time and again, cleverly diverts one from asking such questions (which Nabokov himself would certainly have considered irrelevant and unnecessary). But is this merely a fantastic fantasy, with no other purpose than to be fantastic? (Again, Nabokov would have dismissed such a question.) But we will persist. Does *Pale Fire* have any solid grounding? It certainly does, though they are well obscured by Shade, the Shadows ("a regicidal organization"), and the charades. There are indeed fleeting resemblances to the sober reality of Cornell, Russia, Nabokov's campus life, and so forth, and these provide their own tantalizing conviction to this otherwise apparently lighter-than-air construction. Likewise, the gradual approach of Gradus adds its own heartfelt autobiographical echo.

Nabokov would undoubtedly have been horrified at such an intrusive interpretation. In his view, a work of art should stand on its own, having no other purpose than its own wonderful existence. No nosy investigations are required. In the case of *Pale Fire*, however, such inquiries do add weight to what might otherwise have been mistaken for a somewhat lightweight bauble of genius—all parts and no whole, all art and no heart. The world of *Pale Fire* (the novel) is fantastic, both in its construction and in itself, and the balloon of fantasy does sometimes strain at its anchoring stays. This said, it is difficult not to agree with the assessment of Nabokov's biographer Brian Boyd:

> In sheer beauty of form, *Pale Fire* may well be the most perfect novel ever written. Each scene stands out with crystalline clarity and at the same time flips from right to left, from meaning to madness, in the crazy mirror of Kinbote's mind; each crisp but comically unstable moment challenges us to discover its place in what feigns to be chaos but turns out to be consummate order.

Just two years after the publication of *Pale Fire*, Nabokov's long-completed annotated translation of Pushkin's *Eugene Onegin* appeared, in four hefty volumes. The first volume contained the translator's introduction, followed by the translation itself, which reduced Pushkin's winged poetry to the most pedestrian English prose. Volumes two and three consisted entirely of commentary and appendixes. Volume four contained the index and a photographic reproduction of the original Russian "Evgenii Onegin." In all, these four volumes comprise 1,900 pages, of which just 225 are devoted to the translation of the poem itself.

In the light of *Pale Fire*, this sounds like a colossal, elaborate joke. Edmund Wilson, who had been expecting a serious work, was incensed and wrote a long damning review in the *New York Review of Books*. The tenor of his review can be judged from the following quote:

> Since Mr. Nabokov is in the habit of introducing any job of this kind which he undertakes by an announcement that he is unique and incomparable and that anyone else who has attempted it is an oaf and an ignormaus, incompetent as a linguist and a scholar, usually with the implication that he is also a low-

class person and a ridiculous personality, Nabokov ought not to complain if the reviewer, though trying not to imitate his bad literary manners, does not hesitate to underline his weaknesses.

This signaled the termination of the long friendship between the novelist and the doyen of American critics. Nabokov replied with all guns blazing, referring to Wilson's article:

The mistakes and misstatements in it form an uninterrupted series so complete as to seem artistic in reverse, making one wonder if, perhaps, it had not been woven that way on purpose to be turned into something pertinent and coherent when reflected in a looking glass.

What many failed to realize was that while *Pale Fire* may have been an example of a long joyous joke as literature, Nabokov's translation of *Eugene Onegin* was intended as a work of the highest seriousness. His literal English translation of Pushkin did not reduce the greatest poem in the Russian language to an unpoetic mockery out of vandalistic spite. On the contrary, it sought to convey as far as possible the entire meaning of the original, without any loss that might have occurred by trying to fit the poem into English verse. There was no attempt at poetry: for Nabokov the "poetry" itself remained inseparable from the Russian language in which it was conveyed.

> And you, young beauties, whom
> at a late hour daredevil droshkies
> carry away over the pavement
> of Petersburg

The notes are replete with the extreme pedantry and obscure elucidations, as for instance the following for the above lines:

> The "young beauties," *krasotki molodie*, are courtesans, whom dashing rakes whirl away in light open carriages. This type of carriage came to England, through many stages of transliteration, as a *droitzschka*, but by the 1830's became in London a "drosker" or

"drosky," almost reverting to its native form, *drozhki.* . . .

These lines in fact account for less than half the entire note, which goes on to give no less than three words for "young beauties" that Pushkin used in earlier drafts, as well as telling us where the girls came from (mainly Riga and Warsaw) and solutions to this problem of nomenclature adopted by other "18th century writers, including Karamzin." This note is one of the shorter commentaries.

All this critical apparatus had its own, highly ambitious purpose. The Russia that Nabokov had known in his childhood and early manhood had been overwhelmed by the Soviets, who had done their best to obliterate it, even to the extent of rewriting history. The West had been complicit in this historical vandalism by condemning pre-Soviet Russia as a tyranny not worthy of sympathetic consideration. Nabokov's notes to *Eugene Onegin* were an attempt to re-create and preserve every detail he could remember from the fading picture of Pushkin's world. It was a labor of love, memory, and indefatigable scholarship. Nabokov's estimation of what he had achieved in this work may be gauged by his assertion: "I shall be remembered by *Lolita* and my work on *Eugene Onegin*."

As befits such an ambition, Nabokov's next work of fiction was of great length and even greater ambition. Alas, it would also be his most lightweight. *Ada* (or more fully, *Ada or Ardor: A Family Chronicle*) is a 580-page novel recounting the deep and lasting love of Ada and Van, which begins as a teenage romance and continues long into their old age. It is intended as an enchanting tale, filled with all manner of endearing Nabokovian touches. Ada and Van are brother and sister, and the novel is set in its own beguiling reality. This is called Antiterra, a world which appears much the same as our own, but is altered—almost at whim—to accommodate the author's fantasies—historical, geographical, technological, and so forth. Antiterra has many ironic, jokey resemblances and references to our own world, and at times serves as a semi-metaphorical Russia. The prose that conveys this world and its inhabitants is dense with Nabokovian alliteration, teases, puns, and general trickery—or, perhaps more accurately, tricksiness.

> Sick minds identified the notion of a Terra planet with that of another world and this "Other World" got confused not only with the "Next World" but with the Real World in us and beyond us.

Or:

> Poor Aqua, whose fancies were apt to fall for all the fangles of cranks and Christians, evisaged vividly a minor hymnist's paradise, a future America of alabaster buildings one hundred stories high, resembling a beautiful furniture store crammed with tall whitewashed wardrobes and shorter fridges. . . .

Nabokov attempted to justify all this with some notes which he added to the end of the paperback edition under the name Vivian Darkbloom (an anagram of Vladimir Nabokov), in which he states: "My purpose is not to be facetiously flashy or grotesquely obscure but to express what I feel and think with the utmost truthfulness and perception." The flaw in the novel, and this justification, stems from the last word: "perception." For the most part, perception involves a fixed outer reality. *Ada* consists largely of a world rearranged according to Nabokov's fantasy. Nabokov's vision so overwhelms the world he describes that it becomes entirely his own.

Ada was published in 1969 to huge expectations. It was a Book-of-the-Month Club choice; it was extensively serialized in *Playboy*; a picture of Nabokov appeared on the cover of *Time* magazine; and the movie rights were sold for half a million dollars (with a cleverly negotiated option for Nabokov to raise the price if he felt this was merited). Interviews were sought, and Nabokov conducted these in his customary fashion. The questions were sent to him in advance, and he then composed written answers to those he saw fit to receive such attention. In one answer, he asserted: "I have never seen a more lucid, more lonely, better balanced mind than mine." This pertinently describes the author of *Ada*—though the lucidity might be that of self-reflection, and the loneliness that of the solipsist.

The reviewers of *Ada* were for the most part stunned; and then, belatedly, appalled. Nabokov had at last succumbed to the self-enchantment that had so long threatened to overwhelm his brilliant talent. Nabokov remained aloof. He was by this stage into his seventies. During a visit from his son Dmitri, who had become a well-known opera singer, Nabokov confided that he had now achieved all his dreams as a writer.

Few would deny him this achievement. The author of novels so distinctly Nabokovian and yet so disparate as *The Defense*, *Pnin*, *Lolita*, and *Pale Fire*, the memoirist who gave us *Speak, Memory*, and so much more, could be forgiven his occasional lapses. Few if any other great authors of the twentieth century could lay claim to a body of work containing so many masterpieces. In his use of English, Nabokov had transformed the language, making it utterly his own. It fitted his character like a glove: the complex articulacy of its flourishes and gestures matching perfectly with the complexity of his magical mind. Each sleight of hand fitted each teasing sleight of thought, as tract followed tract, masterpiece followed masterpiece. No list of twentieth-century masters would be complete without him.

Afterword

Vladimir Nabokov died at Montreux in Switzerland on July 2, 1977, at the age of seventy-eight. His wife Vera, his constant companion and chess partner, who had never for a moment doubted his genius and had saved *Lolita* from the flames, lived on for another fourteen years at the Montreux Palace, dying in 1991.

By then the unthinkable had taken place. The Soviet regime had collapsed, and Russia had entered upon the stormy post-revolutionary period which might well have taken place three-quarters of a century earlier if the indecisive but democratic government in which Nabokov's father had served had not been forcibly overthrown by

Lenin. Already Nabokov's personal translation of *Lolita* was freely circulating in the new Russia. Many regarded this work as a national treasure, others found it written in a Russian they found almost impossible to understand. It was "too fancy, and too old-fashioned, like Pushkin." One cannot help feeling that Nabokov would have been particularly pleased by this judgment.

St. Petersburg, after grey years as Petrograd and then Leningrad, has now returned to its former name, though it is no longer the capital. The Nabokov family home on Morskaya (now Herzen) Street still exists, as does the pillared country mansion on the Rozhestveno estate that Nabokov inherited from his uncle Vasily, though the building is now derelict, suffering from the effects of a fire that occurred during the Soviet era.

Nabokov's Chief Works
in English Translation

Alice in Wonderland (1923)‡
Mary (1924)†
King, Queen, Knave (1928)†
The Defense (1930)*†
Laughter in the Dark (1932)†
Despair (1936)†
Invitation to a Beheading (1938)
The Real Life of Sebastian Knight (1941)†
Gogol (1944)*†
Bend Sinister (1947)

*major works
†discussed in text
‡translation

The Gift (1952)
Lolita (1955)*†
Spring in Fialta, and Other Stories (1956)
Pnin (1957)†
Pale Fire (1962)*†
Eugene Onegin: A Novel in Verse by Aleksandr
  Pushkin (1964)*‡
Nabokov's Quartet (1967)
Ada (1969)†
Transparent Things (1972)
Look at the Harlequins! (1974)
Details of a Sunset, and Other Stories (1976)
The Enchanter (1986)†

Chronology of Nabokov's Life and Times

1899	Vladimir Vladimirovich Nabokov born in St. Petersburg, Russia, on April 23 (new-style calendar).
1905	On January 22, "Bloody Sunday," Tsarist soldiers fire on demonstrators outside Winter Palace in St. Petersburg.
1906	Nabokov's father elected to the First State Duma (parliament).
1908	Nabokov's father jailed for three months for defying tsar's decree dissolving the Duma.
1914	Outbreak of World War I. Russia sides with France and Britain against Germany and Austro-Hungary.

1916   Nabokov's uncle dies, leaving him the
        Rozhestveno estate and a considerable
        fortune.

1917   February Revolution. Tsar abdicates.
        Nabokov's father appointed to senior
        position in provisional government.
        November 7 (new style), Lenin and the
        Bolsheviks seize power, and the
        Communist Revolution begins in Russia.
        Nabokov and family move south to
        Crimea, which remains in hands of
        "White" (nonrevolutionary) Russians.
        Russia withdraws from World War I.

1918   End of World War I in Western Europe.

1919   White Army defeated by Red Army in
        Crimea. Nabokov and family flee Russia,
        traveling from Sebastopol via Istanbul
        and Athens to London. Nabokov attends
        Trinity College, Cambridge. Nabokov's
        father and family move to Berlin.

1922   March 28, Nabokov's father assassinated
        at public political meeting. Nabokov
        graduates from Cambridge. Becomes
        engaged to Svetlana Siewert in Berlin.
        Translates *Alice in Wonderland* into
        Russian.

1923   Engagement to Svetlana Siewert broken off. Meets Vera Slonim.

1925   Marries Vera Slonim.

1926   First novel *Mashenka* (Mary) published.

1928   *King, Queen, Knave* published.

1929   *The Defense* first appears in print (serialized in Russian magazine). Wall Street crash plunges world into Great Depression, which lasts through the 1930s. Trotsky banished from Russia, Stalin intensifies collectivization program, bringing famine to the Volga region. Diaghilev dies in Venice, leaving Russian Ballet facing bankruptcy.

1932   Nabokov writes *Despair*.

1933   Hitler comes to power in Germany.

1934   Nabokov's son Dmitri born.

1937   January: Nabokovs leave Germany and settle in France. Nabokov's affair with Irina Guadinini.

1938   Nabokov begins writing first novel in English: *The Real Life of Sebastian Knight*.

1939   Nabokov's mother dies in Prague; Nabokov unable to attend her funeral. Outbreak of World War II in Europe.

1940   Germans invade France. Nabokov and family sail to United States. First meeting with Edmund Wilson.

1941   First appointment at Wellesley College. First drive across America.

1942   Takes on work at the Entomological Museum at Harvard.

1945   Nabokov and his wife become U.S. citizens.

1948   Appointed professor of Russian literature at Cornell.

1953   Finishes writing *Lolita*.

1955   *Lolita* published by Olympia Press in Paris.

1957   Publication of *Pnin*.

1958   *Lolita* finally published in America.

1959   Leaves Cornell. Sails across Atlantic to take up permanent residence in Europe.

1960   Writes screenplay of *Lolita* for Kubrick's film.

1961   Moves into Palace Hotel at Montreux.

1962   Film of *Lolita* opens in New York. *Pale Fire* published.

1964   Publication of Nabokov's translation of *Eugene Onegin* by Pushkin.

1965   Publication of Edmund Wilson's review of *Eugene Onegin*, and spectacular falling out with Nabokov. Nabokov translates *Lolita* into Russian.

1967   Publication of Nabokov's autobiographical *Speak, Memory*.

1974   Publication of *Look at the Harlequins!*

1977   Dies in Switzerland at age seventy-eight.

Recommended Reading

Brian Boyd, *Vladimir Nabokov: The Russian Years* (Princeton University Press, 1993). The first volume of Boyd's exhaustive biography, which makes a valiant attempt to be "definitive." Whether such a thing can be achieved with Nabokov's life is another matter. It contains a huge amount of fascinating material, much of which would not have met with the master's approval.

Brian Boyd, *Vladimir Nabokov: The American Years* (Princeton University Press, 1992). The second volume of Boyd's great biography. Here he is on much firmer American ground, with many living sources and much documentation of this never less than fascinating life.

Andrew Field, *Nabokov: His Life and Art* (Little, Brown, 2000). Field was to become a close friend of Nabokov before the inevitable combustible bust-up. This work of criticism not only shows great insight but also benefits from the author's meetings with Nabokov.

Andrew Field, *VN: The Life and Art of Vladimir Nabokov* (Book Sales, 1992). Andrew Field was daring enough to bring out a critical biography of Nabokov while its subject was still alive, and paid for it with Nabokov's wrath. (Despite Nabokov's fascination with biography in his works, he referred to this genre as "psychoplagiarism," an interesting term which on inspection becomes quite revealing.) Field's second edition of *VN* remains highly complimentary to its subject while revealing a few of the skeletons in the cupboard.

Vladimir Nabokov, *Lectures on Literature* (Harcourt Brace Jovanovich, 1980). These lectures cover several great European figures—such as Kafka, Joyce, and Flaubert—many of whom were favorites of Nabokov. Even so, his "criticism" of their works is never less than oblique, often hilariously so. The sample exam questions at the back are not to be missed.

Vladimir Nabokov, *Lectures on Russian Literature* (Harcourt Brace, 1981). Highly opinionated, not to say eccentric, lectures with which Nabokov baffled his pupils. Expect to be entertained but not to agree. His opinions on writers whom he disliked—such as Dostoevsky—are high comedy.

Vladimir Nabokov, *Speak, Memory: An Autobiography Revisited* (Vintage, 1989). One of Nabokov's finest works of art. But that's just the trouble—as far as autobiography is concerned, it is distinctly selective. Between the floating butterfly lines, however, it is often possible to discern the bee stings inflicted by reality. Either way it is a delight to read, from start to finish (which happens just as he is about to board ship for America).

Vladimir Nabokov, *Strong Opinions* (Vintage, 1990). A collection of various interviews, comments, letters, and articles by Nabokov. With anyone else, such an exercise might appear to be scraping the barrel. But in this case it's from a master stylist—so it's some scraping, some barrel. In Nabokov's interviews the questions were submitted beforehand, and the answers appeared later in written form. As Nabokov himself put it, in this case "interview" should not be mistaken for "a chat between two normal human beings."

Index

A NOTE ON THE AUTHOR

Paul Strathern has lectured in philosophy and mathematics and now lives and writes in London. He is the author of the enormously successful series Philosophers in 90 Minutes. A Somerset Maugham Prize winner, he is also the author of books on history and travel, as well as five novels. His articles have appeared in a great many publications, including the *Observer* (London) and the *Irish Times*.

Paul Strathern's 90 Minutes series in philosophy, also published by Ivan R. Dee, includes individual books on Thomas Aquinas, Aristotle, St. Augustine, Berkeley, Confucius, Derrida, Descartes, Dewey, Foucault, Hegel, Heidegger, Hume, Kant, Kierkegaard, Leibniz, Locke, Machiavelli, Marx, J. S. Mill, Nietzsche, Plato, Rousseau, Bertrand Russell, Sartre, Schopenhauer, Socrates, Spinoza, and Wittgenstein.

NOW PUBLISHED IN THIS SERIES:

Beckett in 90 Minutes
Dostoevsky in 90 Minutes
Kafka in 90 Minutes
D. H. Lawrence in 90 Minutes
Garcia Márquez in 90 Minutes
Nabokov in 90 Minutes

IN PREPARATION:

Jane Austen, Balzac, Bellow, Borges, Brecht,
Camus, Cather, Cervantes, Chekhov, Conrad,
Dante, Dickens, Faulkner, Fitzgerald, Flaubert,
Gogol, Grass, Hardy, Hemingway, Hugo, Huxley,
Ibsen, Henry James, Joyce, Kipling, Mailer, Mann,
Melville, Montaigne, Orwell, Poe, Proust,
Shakespeare, Silone, Singer, Solzhenitsyn, Stendhal,
Stevenson, Tolstoy, Turgenev, Twain, Vonnegut,
Whitman, Virginia Woolf, Zola